Set in the P[...]

Selected by Wendy B[...]

Contents

Section 1

The Paper Bag Princess
by Robert N. Munsch — 2

The Fib
from *The Fib and Other Stories* by George Layton — 5

Section 2

In Search of Gold
from *Shining Rivers* by Ruth Dallas — 9

The Phantom Hound of Yorkshire
from *Amazing True Dog Stories* by Louis Sabin — 15

Section 3

Walk in Backwards…
from *A Dog Called Nelson* by Bill Naughton — 21

The Eagle's Egg
from *Eagle's Egg* by Rosemary Sutcliffe — 27

Edinburgh Gate
Harlow, Essex

The Paper Bag Princess

Elizabeth was a beautiful princess. She lived in a castle and had expensive princess clothes.

She was going to marry a prince named Ronald.

Unfortunately, a dragon smashed her castle, burned all her clothes with his fiery breath, and carried off Prince Ronald.

Elizabeth decided to chase the dragon and get Ronald back.

She looked everywhere for something to wear but the only thing she could find that was not burnt was a paper bag. So she put on the paper bag and followed the dragon.

He was easy to follow because he left a trail of burnt forests and horses' bones.

Finally, Elizabeth came to a cave with a large door that had a huge knocker on it.

She took hold of the knocker and banged on the door.

The dragon stuck his nose out of the door and said, "Well, a princess! I love to eat princesses, but I have already eaten a whole castle today. I am a very busy dragon. Come back tomorrow."

He slammed the door so fast that Elizabeth almost got her nose caught.

Elizabeth grabbed the knocker and banged on the door again.

The dragon stuck his nose out of the door and said, "Go away. I love to eat princesses, but I have already eaten a whole castle today. I am a very busy dragon. Come back tomorrow."

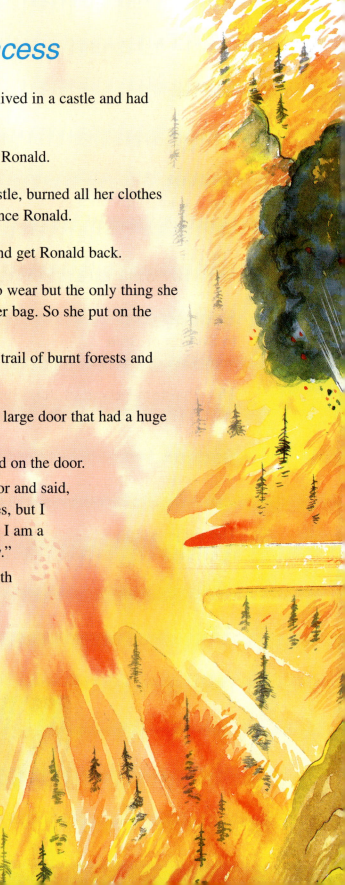

"Wait," shouted Elizabeth. "Is it true that you are the smartest and fiercest dragon in the whole world?"

"Yes," said the dragon.

"Is it true," said Elizabeth, "that you can burn up ten forests with your fiery breath?"

"Oh, yes," said the dragon, and he took a huge, deep breath and breathed out so much fire that he burnt up fifty forests.

"Fantastic," said Elizabeth, and the dragon took another huge breath and breathed out so much fire that he burnt up one hundred forests.

"Magnificent," said Elizabeth, and the dragon took another huge breath, but this time nothing came out.

The dragon didn't even have enough fire left to cook a meatball.

Elizabeth said, "Dragon, is it true that you can fly around the world in just ten seconds?"

"Why, yes," said the dragon and jumped up and flew all the way around the world in just ten seconds.

He was very tired when he got back, but Elizabeth shouted, "Fantastic, do it again!"

So the dragon jumped up and flew around the whole world in just twenty seconds.

When he got back he was too tired to talk and he lay down and went straight to sleep.

Elizabeth whispered very softly, "Hey, dragon." The dragon didn't move at all.

She lifted up the dragon's ear and put her head right inside. She shouted as loud as she could, "Hey, dragon!"

The dragon was so tired he didn't even move.

Elizabeth walked right over the dragon and opened the door to the cave.

There was Prince Ronald.

He looked at her and said, "Elizabeth, you are a mess! You smell like ashes, your hair is all tangled and you are wearing a dirty old paper bag. Come back when you are dressed like a real princess."

"Ronald," said Elizabeth. "Your clothes are really pretty and your hair is very neat. You look like a real prince, but you are a toad."

They didn't get married after all.

By Robert N. Munsch

The Fib

Back in the changing room, Gordon started going on about my football kit. He egged everybody else on.

"Listen, Barraclough, this strip belonged to my uncle and he scored thousands of goals."

Gordon just laughed.

"Your uncle? Your auntie more like. You look like a big girl."

"Listen, Barraclough, you don't know who my uncle is."

I was sick of Gordon Barraclough. I was sick of his bullying and his shouting, and his crawling round Melrose. And I was sick of him being a good footballer.

"My uncle is Bobby Charlton!"

That was the fib.

For a split second I think Gordon believed me, then he burst out laughing. So did everyone else. Even Tony laughed.

"Bobby Charlton – your uncle? You don't expect us to believe that, do you?"

"Believe what you like, it's the truth."

Of course they didn't believe me. That's why the fib became a lie.

"Cross my heart and hope to die."

I spat on my left hand. They all went quiet. Gordon put his face close to mine.

"You're a liar."

I was.

"I'm not. Cross my heart and hope to die."

I spat on my hand again. If I'd dropped dead on the spot, I wouldn't have been surprised. Thank goodness Melrose came in, and made us hurry onto the bus.

Gordon and me didn't talk to each other much for the rest of the day. All afternoon I could see him looking at me. He was so sure I was a liar, but he just couldn't be certain.

Why had I been so daft as to tell such a stupid lie? Well, it was only a fib really, and at least it shut Gordon Barraclough up for an afternoon.

After school, Tony and me went into town to watch the lights being switched on. Norbert tagged along as well. He'd forgotten all about his trouble with Melrose that morning. He's like that, Norbert. Me, I would've been upset for days.

There was a crowd at the bottom of the Town Hall steps, and we managed to get right to the front. Gordon was there already. Norbert was ready for another fight, but we stopped him. When the Lord Mayor came out we all clapped. He had his chain on, and he made a speech about the Christmas appeal.

Then it came to switching on the lights.

"... and as you know, ladies and gentlemen, boys and girls, we always try to get someone special to switch on our Chamber of Commerce Christmas lights, and this year is no exception. Let's give a warm welcome to Mr Bobby Charlton..."

I couldn't believe it. I nearly fainted. I couldn't move for a few minutes. Everybody was asking for his autograph. When it was Gordon's turn, I saw him pointing at me. I could feel myself going red. Then, I saw him waving me over. Not Gordon, Bobby Charlton!

I went. Tony and Norbert followed. Gordon was grinning at me.

"You've had it now. You're for it now. I told him you said he's your uncle."

I looked up at Bobby Charlton. He looked down at me. I could feel my face going even redder. Then suddenly, he winked at me and smiled.

"Hello, son. Aren't you going to say hello to your Uncle Bobby, then?"

I couldn't believe it. Neither could Tony or Norbert. Or Gordon.

"Er ... hello ... Uncle ... er ... Bobby."

He ruffled my hair.

"How's your mam?"

"All right."

He looked at Tony, Norbert and Gordon.

"Are these your mates?"

"These two are."

I pointed out Tony and Norbert.

"Well, why don't you bring them in for a cup of tea?"

I didn't understand.

"In where?"

"Into the Lord Mayor's Parlour. For tea. Don't you want to come?"

"Yeah, that'd be lovely ... Uncle Bobby."

Uncle Bobby! I nearly believed it myself. And I'll never forget the look on Gordon Barraclough's face as Bobby Charlton led Tony, Norbert and me into the Town Hall.

It was ever so posh in the Lord Mayor's Parlour. We had sandwiches without crusts, malt loaf and butterfly cakes. It was smashing. So was Bobby Charlton. I just couldn't believe we were there. Suddenly, Tony kept trying to tell me something, but I didn't want to listen to him. I wanted to listen to Bobby.

"Shurrup, I'm trying to listen to my Uncle Bobby."

"But do you know what time it is? Six o'clock!"

"Six o'clock! Blimey! I've got to get going. My mum'll kill me."

I said goodbye to Bobby Charlton.

"Tarah, Uncle Bobby. I've got to go now. Thanks …"

He looked at me and smiled.

"Tarah, son. See you again some time."

When we got outside, Tony and Norbert said it was the best tea they'd ever had.

I ran home as fast as I could. My mum was already in, of course. I was hoping she wouldn't be too worried. Still, I knew everything would be all right once I'd told her I was late because I'd been having tea in the Lord Mayor's Parlour with Bobby Charlton.

"Where've you been? It's gone quarter past six. I've been worried sick."

"It's all right, Mum. I've been having tea in the Lord Mayor's Parlour with Bobby Charlton ..."

She gave me such a clout, I thought my head was going to fall off. My mum never believes me, even when I'm telling the truth!

**From *The Fib and Other Stories*
By George Layton**

In Search of Gold

Fourteen-year-old Johnie has teamed up with an old digger called Tatey in search of gold.

My thoughts raced round in my head, wondering whether I should tell Dan or not tell Dan, blaming myself for not hiding the gold in a better place, growing full of anger against the person who had taken the gold that had cost me a hard week's work, and, most of all, blaming myself for leaving the camp at all. I also felt that I had let Tatey down, because he had left me in charge and told me to look after the tent and the claim, and when he came back I would have no gold to show him, just as though I had loafed the whole week.

I grew very miserable after an hour of these thoughts, and realised that there was nothing at all I could do as I hadn't a shred of proof against anyone. And even if I could find out who had my gold what could a boy do against men? It was true, as Dan had always told me, I was too young for the goldfields.

In this mood of despondency I went to bed without bothering to eat anything, having lost my appetite, and shed a few tears into the red scarf my mother had knitted for me, before falling asleep.

I was awakened by a slight sound outside the tent when it was still dark. A black figure filled the tent-opening and approached me and I sat up, terrified, thinking someone was going to kill me.

"Not a sound!" hissed a voice. It was Tatey.

My heart was banging so loudly that I thought he must hear it.

"Johnie!" He moved close to my ear. "I've found gold. I had to wait till it was dark to come in. I don't want to be followed. Get up and put on all the warm clothes you've got. Spread out your blanket and put in all the food. We'll take the frying pan and not another thing. I've left my gear over the hills. We'll leave the tent standing – everything. Just take what you can carry. I'm going to carry the cradle."

"It's too heavy," I whispered, awed by his whispering voice, and sensing his excitement.

"There's no coming back," Tatey said. "What we take now is all we're going to have. So use your wits."

"I had two ounces of gold," I told him, "and someone has taken it."

After a moment's pause Tatey said, "That's chicken-feed where we're going." When I heard that, all my troubles fell away from me. I got up in the greatest of excitement and bundled up a heavy swag as Tatey directed me, all in no more light than came from the moon and stars, and like two shadows we stole away from Gabriels' Gully, with Tatey actually carrying the heavy gold-cradle on his back. We left our tent standing as though still occupied.

Travelling by night was very slow, but gradually the sky lightened and the sun came up in a clear sky and shone on the tops of the hills that surrounded us. There was no road, no track, no fence, no house, no tree in that lonely landscape. The only vegetation was the New Zealand tussock and thorny bushes which grew among great rough rocks.

Tatey wanted to put the greatest distance possible between ourselves and the gully we had left, so we kept on till I felt my legs trembling from hunger and weariness and asked him when we were going to have breakfast. We had climbed down into a pass, by that time, where a little stream ran over stones, and there, hidden between two great rocks as big as houses, we fried some bacon in the pan and then boiled water in the same pan and drank it scalding hot. Tatey took care to hide the evidence of our fire and we pressed on, sleeping that night in the tussocks in the shelter of rocks.

Rocks had become the main feature of the landscape, some standing in clusters as though meeting to discuss the intrusion of two fly-like human beings on their territory. Some were in long ridges, like petrified railway carriages. Some had mats of tussock on their heads like wigs. It was desert country, steep country, a mad kind of country, only fit for madmen in search of gold.

Tatey was a little ahead of me. I was tramping along behind him. At the top of a hill he paused and told me to look down. In the next valley I could see the gleam of water like a knife blade. A stream wound along the valley floor, a mere ribbon of water, running over a wide area of bare mountain shingle, sometimes hidden, and sometimes showing up further on.

"No one's been here," Tatey said, "ever." And he began to hurry down the steep hillside as though in competition with other men who might reach the stream first.

"This is the spot," he said, setting down the cradle at the waterside. I, too, set down my swag, and was very glad to do so. I could see no sign of Tatey's having staked out a claim, or of a pit where he had been digging. The stony valley was bare and desolate and we were enclosed by a complete circle of bare hills. The water made a musical sound as it ran over the stones. To my great amazement Tatey seized the frying pan and walked into the water without taking his boots off, and, with his bare hands, began to scoop gravel from the bottom of the river into the pan, and to wash it, where he stood. Then he carried the pan out to me and I could see gold shining on the bottom as though it had been spilt there.

We stared at the gold and looked into each other's faces, neither of us able to speak. I had imagined that men jumped for joy when they found gold. Instead, I found tears blurring my vision.

**From *Shining Rivers*
By Ruth Dallas**

The Phantom Hound of Yorkshire

The night of February 6, 1854, seemed to be made for "the devil's work". It was bitterly cold and windy. Thick clouds rode the sky, and the pale moon shone fitfully.

On this winter's night, the good Mr Woodcock was taking home two large sacks. One held important papers; the other held a large amount of money. He had strung the sacks across his shoulders by a heavy cord, and they bounced against his sides as he walked.

He was not armed. He was well protected, he said, "by the Good Book I carry with me everywhere". He kept it handy in his coat pocket.

As the fearless clergyman walked along the dark road, he quoted biblical verses to himself. It made the time pass more easily. A light snow began to fall. In the cloudy light, the silvery snow gave an eerie glow to the trees and shrubs on both sides of the road.

Mr Woodcock heard an owl hoot close by. A moment later, the voice of another owl answered from deep in the surrounding woods. "At least," the clergyman told himself, "I think those are owls I hear."

Just then the clouds parted, and the landscape was bathed in brilliant moonlight. This was followed by a few seconds of silence. It was finally broken by the steady beat of footsteps. They were coming from somewhere behind the clergyman. The footsteps came faster and faster, closer and closer.

Mr Woodcock stopped and wheeled around. "Who is there?" he called out.

And from out of a thin mist swirling behind him, a giant hound padded into the moonlight. It had a thick, uncombed coat of grey fur. It stood about level with the clergyman's chest, and he was a man about two metres tall. But what captured his attention was the huge creature's eyes. They glowed with what he called "a white fire", like two small moons under a thin film of clouds.

This strange animal padded right up to the clergyman, but Mr Woodcock was unafraid. He put out his hand to the dog, and the animal showed only friendliness. The large, rough tongue licked one of the clergyman's hands. At the same time, the dog turned its weird eyes up to stare at the man. They looked at each other for a long moment. Then, as if by agreement, they began to walk along the road. The dog stayed just to the right of the good man, never falling behind or going ahead.

Less than fifteen minutes passed, when the dog's behaviour suddenly changed. It moved into the lead by several metres. Then, looking back as if to check on the clergyman's safety, it left the road and trotted along the shadowy line of trees.

All of a sudden the dog was gone, swallowed by the trees and darkness. Mr Woodcock came to a halt, listening. There was no sound at all – not even the normal whistles and snapping twigs and other night sounds of birds and animals that are active in the dark hours. "It was a most unnatural silence," the clergyman said later. "It was as if I had entered another world."

Then the dog reappeared. Moving low to the ground, it came out of the woods and right up to the man. But it suddenly whirled toward the woods again and began to growl, a deep rumbling in its thick chest.

Now the clergyman heard a new sound. It was a brushing sound, such as clothing makes when it rubs against brush and branches. He turned in the direction it came from. As he did so, he caught a glimpse of three men slipping in and out of the shadows. The dog seemed rooted where it stood. It continued to growl menacingly at the spot where those men had been.

Mr Woodcock patted the dog and started walking along the road again. It was growing late. His family would soon begin to worry about him. He didn't want them wandering about on a night like this, hunting for him.

Man and dog had travelled no more than another hundred metres when the deep growls started again. Again Mr Woodcock searched in the direction the dog was facing. The moon was out now, and he saw, outlined against the sky, the same three men. They had come out of the woods and were standing farther down the road, waiting.

The dog leapt into a run, directly for the men. They broke for the cover of the trees. Soon the clergyman could hear branches cracking as they plunged deeper into the woods.

Mr Woodcock caught up with the dog. "The quicker we get away from this place, the better," he said to his furry companion. And he set off at a good pace, the dog trotting alongside.

The would-be thieves were seen three more times by the clergyman as he made his way along the wooded path. Each time they seemed about to come at him. And one time he thought he saw weapons – guns and knives – in their hands. But each time they came out of hiding they were frightened off by Mr Woodcock's growling guardian.

"However much they wanted the money at my side," the clergyman remarked, "they were not willing to risk the fury of my companion to come after it."

At long last, the walk ended as the clergyman reached his home. Standing just a few metres from the front door, Mr Woodcock beckoned to the dog to come inside. "I will feed you," the man said.

The dog moved close to the clergyman. He licked the man's hand just the way he had before. He gazed at the man with those twin-moon eyes, barked softly one time – and vanished.

The Reverend Isaac Woodcock told the events of that fantastic night again and again, until the end of his life. He believed firmly that it had all happened just the way he remembered it. He talked to everyone who lived within several kilometres of his home, asking about the phantom of the night. Nobody knew of such an animal. Not one person had ever seen or heard about a dog anything like that one.

They were sure that the clergyman's life – and the church's money – had been saved that night by a supernatural creature. In time, the clergyman came to share their feelings. And every time he walked the road that wound through the dark woods, he kept a sharp lookout for his phantom friend. The dog never reappeared. But then, Mr Woodcock was never again followed by thieves!

**From *Amazing True Dog Stories*
By Louis Sabin**

Walk In Backwards …

A visit to the pictures in those days was different from today. For a start there were two houses – that is to say, the First House emptied and the Second House came in. This meant they could take more money at the box office. Also, you were never interrupted during a film with people coming and going.

It was often very hard to raise the twopence needed to go to the First House, and there was a great deal of what was known as *pinching in*. Now the way to go about that was to *walk in backwards* and pretend you were going out. That is to say, if you had no money, you would hang around outside the big exit doors until the First House was over and you heard the bolts being drawn and the doors opening.

As the doors opened the rush of patrons would issue forth, their faces flushed and their eyes often red. Those early films flickered so much that you could not watch long without your eyes showing the strain. That was your moment for sneaking in. But it was no use going in facing the mob coming out, for you'd get swept backwards and off your feet. So what you had to do was turn your back on the mob and force your way backwards inside the cinema. If anybody said anything to you – "Out the flamin' way," or anything of that sort – you simply said, "Sorry – but I've forgotten my cap." That was sort of making out you had already been inside.

Getting inside was only half the battle, for they wouldn't let the new customers in at the paybox until they were sure, or thought they were sure, that everybody was outside. But the smell of the inside of the Derby Picture Palace, which was a musty mixture of films, people, tobacco smoke and orange peel, would so excite a lad that he would do almost anything rather than be turned out. You could hide under the seats, or sneak up behind the piano, or dodge under a curtain or slip into the toilets and climb on top and lie down on top of a lavatory, so that no one could see you, and then quietly move into a seat once the Second House patrons had begun to move in. It wasn't easy. But it was very exciting.

Nelson [the dog] was not one to be left out of the fun and, no matter what watch was placed on the doors, Nelson would find his way in. The owner of the Derby Picture Palace in those days was a man called Tutty Booth. He was quite a nice chap, really, with wavy ginger hair. Everybody to do with pictures seemed to have wavy hair, for the woman in the paybox had wavy hair, and so had the operator. But Tutty Booth could not stand old Nelson. The reason was simple. We boys went in the Tuppennies. They were not individual seats, of course, but just rows of wooden benches. And you had bare wooden boards under your feet. As soon as the lights went down old Nelson would find his way in and come straight to us in the dark. He liked sitting on my lap, but he was a bit of a weight, and we used to spread him out a bit between two or three of us.

Nelson enjoyed Charlie Chaplin comedies, and especially all the kicking up the backside that went on in them. But his favourite films were what are now called *Westerns*, but were then known as *Cowboy films*. What he couldn't stand were *society dramas*, films all about toffs, in which the men wore evening dress most of the time and looked right cissies, and the women had long gowns and lots of necklaces, and they sort of gaped at one another making out they were in love. Anything to do with what they called love used to bore old Nelson stiff. You could tell almost from the start when a film was going to be no good, but it seemed the audience would hang on, hoping for something to happen.

It was an understood thing amongst us lads that any mate who had got up early, say a little-piecer in the mill or a lad who went round with papers and had to be up about half past five every morning, could work in a little kip. He would rest his head down on the back of the wooden seat in front of him, or even on someone's lap. "Wakken me up when something happens," he would say, "– or when this is over an' the comic starts."

As soon as old Nelson spotted this he would join in, for he just couldn't stand the actors looking ga-ga at one another, and he would look round for a handy shoulder, arm or knee to get his head down on, and at the same time he would let out one of those long loud yawns that some dogs are very good at. If the yawn didn't set the audience off, very soon his snores would. As Pongo used to say, they didn't sound like dog snores but more like some prehistoric animal frightening off all intruders.

The films were silent of course, except for this grating buzz from the projection box, and it seems that Nelson would wait until the woman who played the piano had stopped to rest her fingers for a few moments. She used to play "In a Monastery Garden" for religious scenes, and if there was a chase with horses she would play a galloping march, and in time her fingers seemed to get cramp or something, and she would stop playing and rub them. It would be just that moment of silence when Nelson would let out one or two of his loudest snores, and follow up quickly with some long, weird, whining moans, that sounded as though they might be coming from a dog stranded on some wild, lonely shore, and threatened with a slow, lingering death from sheer boredom.

Any trickle of interest the film may have had would be slashed stone dead at the sound of that great snoring moan from Nelson. Folk could hear it away back in the posh tanner seats. Then somebody would laugh. And that would set the lot off. Then the youngsters in their clogs would start stamping on the wooden floor and at the same time yelling out: "Take it off, Tutty! Take it off!" What with the stamping and yelling the place would be in an uproar, and the film would have to stop and the lights come on. Tutty Booth would attempt to address the audience from the stage but no one would listen: "Send for a cowboy film!" they would yell. "We're not paying good money to watch that sort of stuff." Then someone would shout: "Why, even the dog went to sleep!"

So what would happen then would be that the boring film would be taken off, a short comic film put on, until Tutty Booth had borrowed a film from another cinema. "If only I could find that dog," he used to say. "They would never have known but for him."

**From *A Dog Called Nelson*
By Bill Naughton**

The Eagle's Egg

Quintus, the storyteller, is a standard bearer in the Ninth Legion of the Roman army, which is fighting against the Picts under the leadership of General Agricola.

I began to smell trouble coming, sure as acorns grow on oak trees. And then one day when we had almost won through to spring, some of the men broke into the wine store and were found drunk on watch. They were put under guard, ready to be brought up before the Senior Centurion next day. And everyone knew what that meant. He'd have been within his rights to order the death penalty, but being Daddy Dexius, who could be relied on to be soft in such matters, they would probably get off with a flogging. Even so, it would be the kind of flogging that spreads a man flat on his face in the sick block for three days afterwards.

All the rest of that day you could feel the trouble like nearing thunder prickling in the back of your neck. And in the middle of supper, it came.

Being the Eagle bearer, I ate in the Centurions' mess-hall, though in the lowest place there, next to the door, and I hadn't long sat down when the noise began.

It wasn't particularly loud, but there was an ugly note to it, a snarling note, and in the midst of it someone shouting, "Come on, lads, let's get the prisoners out!" and other voices taking up the cry.

I remember Dexius's face as he got up and strode past me to the door, and suddenly knowing that we had all been quite wrong about him, that he wasn't soft at all. More the kind of man who gets a reputation for being good-tempered and fair-game, because he knows that if he once lets his temper go and hits somebody he probably won't leave off till he's killed them.

I had only just started my supper, so I snatched a hard-boiled duck's egg from a bowl on the table and shoved it down the front of my uniform, and dashed out with the rest.

Outside on the parade-ground a crowd was gathering. Some of them had makeshift torches. The flare of them was teased by the thin wind that was blowing, and their light fell ragged on faces that were sullen and dangerous. Vipsanius the duty centurion was trying to deal with the situation, but he didn't seem to be having much success, and the crowd was getting bigger every moment.

Daddy Dexius said coolly, "What goes on here, Centurion?"

"They're refusing to go on watch, Sir," said Vipsanius. I mind he was sweating up a bit, despite the edge to the wind.

"We've had enough of going on watch in this dog-hole, night after filthy night!" someone shouted.

And his mates backed him up. "How much longer are we going to squat here, making a free target of ourselves for the blue painted barbarians?"

"If Agricola wants to fight them, why doesn't he come up and get things going?"

"Otherwise why don't we get out of here and go back where we came from?"

Men began shouting from all over the crowd, bringing up all the old soldiers' grievances about pay and leave and living conditions. "We've had enough!" they shouted, "We've had enough!"

"You'll have had more than enough, and the Painted People down on us, if you don't break up and get back on duty!" Vipsanius yelled back at them.

But the sullen crowd showed no sight of breaking up or getting back on duty. And suddenly, only half-believing, I understood just how ugly things might be going to turn. Not much harm done up to now, but if something, anything, tipped matters even a little in the wrong direction, the whole crowd could flare up into revolt, and revolt has a way of spreading that puts a heath-fire to shame.

Centurion Dexius said, "Thank you, Centurion, I will take over now." And then he glanced round for me. "Standard-bearer."

"Here, Sir," says I, advancing smartly.

"Go and fetch out the Eagle, and we'll see if that will bring them to their senses."

I left him standing there, not trying to shout them down or anything, just standing there, and went to fetch the Eagle.

In the Saccellum, part office and part treasury and part shrine, the lamp was burning on the table where the duty centurion would sit all night with his drawn sword before him – when not doing rounds or out trying to quell a riot – and the Eagle on its tall shaft stood against the wall, with the Cohort standards ranged on either side of it.

I took it down and, as I did so, its upward shadow, cast by the lamp on the table engulfed half the chamber behind it, as though some vast dark bird had spread wing and come swooping forward out of the gloom among the rafters. Used though I was to the Eagle standard, that great swoop of dark wings made me jump half out of my skin. But it was not the moment to be having fancies. I hitched up the Eagle into Parade Position, and out I went with it.

The Senior Centurion had quieted them down a bit – well, the look on his face would have quieted all Rome on a feast day – and when they saw the Eagle, their growling and muttering died away till I could hear a fox barking, way up the valley, and the vixen's scream in answer. But they still stood their ground, and I knew the quiet wouldn't last. And there was I, standing up with the Eagle, not knowing quite what to do next and, truth to tell, beginning to feel a bit of a fool. And then suddenly it came to me, what I had to do next, and I pulled out the duck's egg from inside my tunic and held it up.

And, "Now look what you've done, you lot!" said I, "Behaving like this you've upset the Eagle so much it's laid an egg!"

I have noticed more than once in the years since then, that it is sometimes easier to swing the mood of a whole crowd than it is to swing the mood of one man on his own. Aye, a dicey thing is a crowd.

There was a moment of stunned silence, and then someone laughed, and someone else took up the laugh, and then more and more, a roar of laughter and a surge of stamping and back-slapping that swept away all that had gone before.

**From *Eagle's Egg*
By Rosemary Sutcliffe**